DIVE
TO THE
CORAL
REEFS

DIVE TO THE CORAL REEFS

A NEW ENGLAND AQUARIUM BOOK

written by Elizabeth Tayntor,
Paul Erickson and Les Kaufman

CROWN PUBLISHERS, INC.
NEW YORK

Published by Crown Publishers, Inc. 225 Park Avenue South,
New York, New York 10003

CROWN is a trademark of Crown Publishers, Inc.

Manufactured in Japan

Design by Kathleen Westray and Ed Sturmer,
Design and Printing Productions, New York City.

Library of Congress Cataloging-in-Publication Data

Dive to the coral reefs.
"A New England Aquarium book."
Summary: Describes the formation of coral reefs
and the many plants and animals that live in
and around these underwater communities.
1. Coral reef biology—Juvenile literature.
2. Coral reefs and islands—Juvenile literature.
[1. Coral reef biology. 2. Coral reefs and islands]
I. New England Aquarium
QH95.8.D59   574.5′26367   86-4565

ISBN 0-517-56311-8

10 9 8 7 6 5 4 3 2 1

First Edition

PHOTO CREDITS:
Animals, Animals: pp. 11 (bottom), 12.
Fred Bavendam: pp. 11 (top), 14 (left), 16, 21, 25, 28.
Nick Coloyianis: p. 5
Chris Newbert: cover, pp. 3, 6, 7, 8, 10, 13, 14 (right),
    15 (bottom), 19, 20, 22, 26, 27, 28, 29, 30, 31, 32, 33,
    35 (top), 36.
Dr. James Porter: pp. 34, 35 (bottom).
George Sheng: p. 24.
Alese and Morton Pechter: back cover

Did you know that there is a city full of fantastic shapes and structures that lies beneath the surface of the sea? It is a city few people have seen because it is so difficult to reach.

Yet it is one of the largest, most colorful, most amazing communities in the world. It is built and inhabited by millions of incredible creatures. It is the living coral reef.

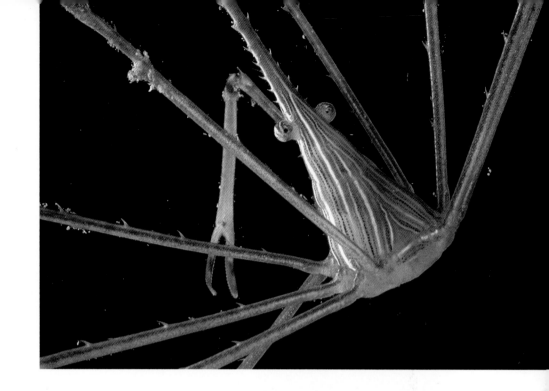

Coral reefs grow in tropical oceans all over the
world. The largest, over 1,200 miles long, is the Great
Barrier Reef off the coast of Australia. To find out
about these underwater coral communities, the New
England Aquarium sent a team of scientists and divers
to the island of Jamaica in the Caribbean Sea. Their
mission: to explore the legendary Pear Tree and Rio
Bueno reefs off the island's north coast.

Down here, the coral grows nearly the whole length of the island, from east to west. It rises 40 feet above the sea floor. The divers explored reef growth more than 5,000 years old.

Reefs are built very, very slowly, by corals: tiny animals that actually make up the mounds, boulders, and branches called a coral reef. For example, a mound of brain coral, 3 feet tall, may be 250 years old.

Each coral animal, or polyp, is about the size of a pencil eraser.

A coral polyp has a soft body, stomach, and mouth surrounded by tentacles. Corals are hunters. Like their cousins, the jellyfishes, they use their tentacles to capture their prey, small drifting plants and animals called plankton.

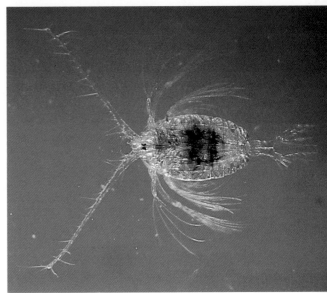

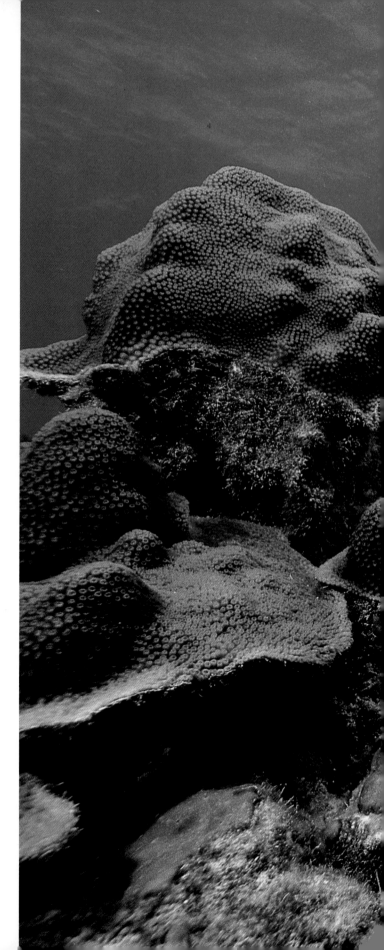

Some people are surprised to find out that corals are animals because many look more like plants. There is something amazing about corals that helps to explain their plantlike shapes. Scientists have discovered that coral animals are also part plant.

Imagine tiny green plants growing under your skin. Corals have tiny plants, called zooxanthellae, growing inside of them. Like other plants, zooxanthellae use the sun to make food through a process called photosynthesis. Then they pass some of this food on to the coral polyps, and this helps the coral grow.

Each coral polyp uses
minerals from seawater to
build a limestone skeleton.
When disturbed, polyps
can pull into the protection
of these hard, rocklike homes.

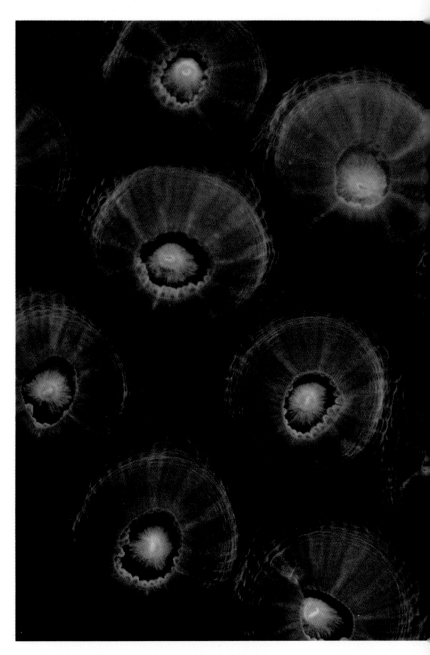

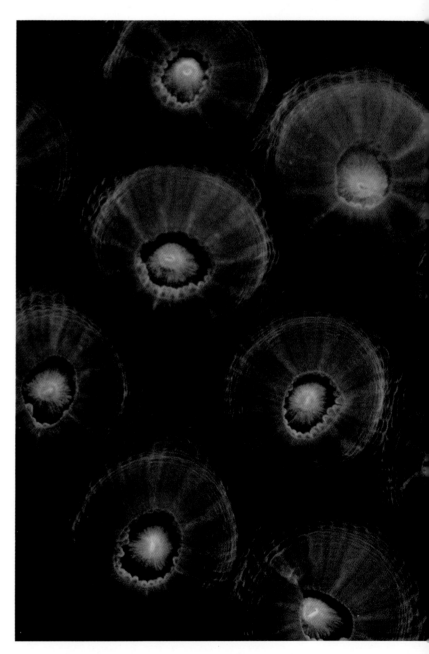

Each coral polyp uses
minerals from seawater to
build a limestone skeleton.
When disturbed, polyps
can pull into the protection
of these hard, rocklike homes.

When we think of coral, we often picture the hard white skeletons of corals that have died. Polyps, like people, live close together in colonies. As polyps grow, they move up to build new skeletons on top of the old. And, very slowly, the reef grows with them. It's like a modern city built upon the ruins of an ancient civilization.

Hundreds of individuals make up the forms of the reef. Different species of coral form different shapes.

Staghorn coral looks like deer antlers.

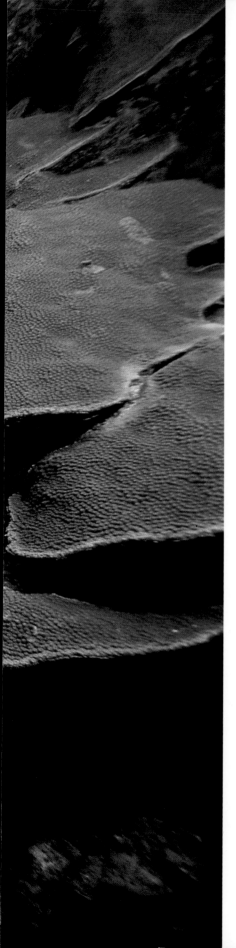

You can see how plate coral gets its name. It is big and flat, like a giant dinner plate.

Brain coral looks like the surface of a human brain with furrows and ridges.

These corals build hard skeletons. . . .

But sea fans, sea whips, and other soft corals have flexible skeletons. In ocean currents, soft corals bend and sway like tree branches in a heavy breeze.

The reef is home to literally millions of plants and animals because it offers good feeding and good places to hide. Small reef dwellers need protection from the many hunters of the reef.

Larger fishes probe cracks and holes in the reef, looking for tasty crabs and worms.

Butterflyfishes are especially good at this because they have long snouts and they can reach into places other fishes can't.

But in no time at all, the tables can turn and hunters become the hunted, victims of larger predators like the great barracuda. This fish grows to 6 feet in length and attacks its prey with lightning speed.

The great barracuda was curious about the divers, following them for a long time. But despite its curiosity, the big fish is not likely to attack snorkelers and divers.

The reef is a feeding ground for a variety of sharks. This shark has 7 rows of sharp teeth for hunting. When a tooth from the front row falls out, one from behind moves up to take its place. Though sharks do not hunt people for food, divers are cautious and give them plenty of room.

As they snorkeled over the reef, the divers saw nurse sharks resting on the sand. Nurse sharks feed on spiny lobsters and crabs. They act like underwater vacuum cleaners. They move close to a hole and suck their victims right out of hiding places in the reef.

The divers surprised a sea turtle who was sleeping under a
ledge. Like humans, sea turtles need to come up for air. But unlike
people, these turtles can hold their breath for up to 2 hours.

Animals and plants are everywhere on the reef. Every inch of space is used by living things. Some animals even live inside other animals: shrimp in sponges, and worms in coral.

These snapping shrimp are just two of dozens that were living inside a sponge. To defend itself, the shrimp uses its large claw to make a loud snapping sound that startles nearby hungry predators.

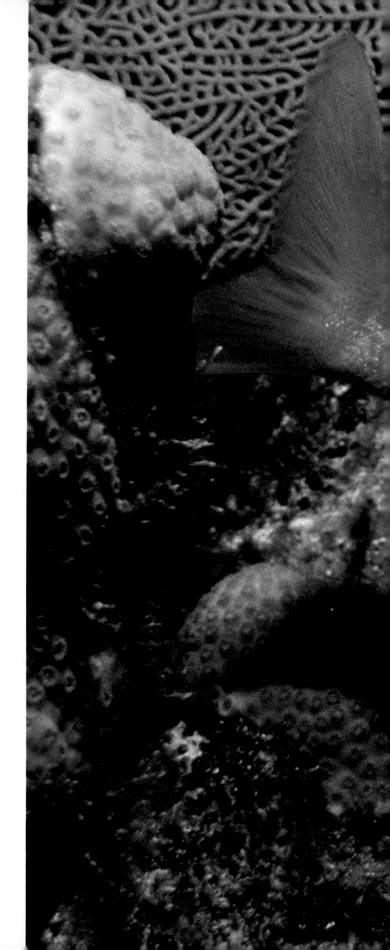

Exploring the shallow reef was just one part of the New England Aquarium dive team's job. Next they dove the deep reef. The divers dropped off the reef edge and descended 100 feet down the reef wall. Special training is required to make a dive like this and it challenges even experts!

One of the divers describes how it feels to dive the deep reef: "Diving the reef wall is like flying off the side of a mountain with a thousand feet of open water below you."

As the divers went deeper, it got darker.

At about 60 feet, they looked into a crack in the reef, and an octopus came shooting out and draped itself over the corals. Frightened, the octopus changed colors. These camouflage experts are shy animals and it is rare to see one in the open.

At 80 feet down the divers entered a long cave . . . and came out 100 feet below the water's surface.

Here it feels like being on another planet. Enormous sponges grow
out of the reef wall. Some are so large a diver can stand inside.

A green moray eel stared out from its underwater cave. By day these fish hide, waiting for something to come a little bit too close. Then they lunge out at it with their sharp teeth. At night they may hunt for octopus and lobsters.

The divers were amazed by the beauty of the reef and the number of organisms that live there. Because everything fits together like a puzzle, one change can create problems for everyone.

In the coral reefs, natural as well as human disasters cause destruction. Dense thickets of staghorn coral are often victims of hurricanes. Despite their hard skeletons, stony corals are surprisingly fragile and easily damaged by anchor-dragging boats. Souvenir collectors destroy living coral that may be decades old.

Probably the greatest threat to corals is coastline development. Offshore oil spills and open ocean dumping may destroy large areas of the reef forever.

Coral reefs can only be preserved through wise ocean management.
So maybe someday you, too, can put on scuba tanks and explore this
fantastic underwater world.